CONTENTS

THE COMPLETE COWBOY BUCKET LIST

100 Cowboy Things to Do Before You Put Your Horse Up and Go to the House

by **Slim Randles**

with A Few Words by Johnny D. Boggs

Río Grande Books
Los Ranchos, NM

For Gene and Lona and Rocky and Steve and Dick and Roy and Hap and Slim N. — Thanks

The Bucket List Book Series

The Complete Cowboy Bucket List by Slim Randles
The Ultimate Hot Air Balloon Bucket List by Barbe Awalt
The Basic New Mexico Bucket List by Barbe Awalt

The Complete Space Buff's Bucket List by Loretta Hall (2016)
The Complete Crab Lovers' Bucket List by Barbe Awalt (2016)
The Complete Green Chile Cheesburger Lovers' Bucket List by Barbe Awalt (2016)

Published by Río Grande Books
925 Salamanca NW, Los Ranchos, NM 87107-5647
505-344-9382 www.RioGrandeBooks.com

Printed in the United States of America Book Design: Paul Rhetts

Library of Congress Cataloging-in-Publication Data

Randles, Slim, author.
The cowboy bucket list : 100 cowboy things to do before you put your horse up and go to the house / Slim Randles.
pages cm
ISBN 978-1-936744-38-1 (pbk. : alk. paper)
1. Cowboys--Miscellanea. 2. Ranch life--West (U.S.)--Miscellanea. 3. West (U.S.)--Miscellanea. I. Title.
F596.R3585 2015
978--dc23
2015023796

Front cover: Old Barn wood wall (Courtesy of Paul Rhetts); Back cover: Rack of cowboy boots (Courtesy of Wikipedia) and Slim Randles with his dutch oven in Chama, NM (Courtesy of the author).

Slim on a photo pony in Los Angeles, age 4. *Courtesy of the author.*

Riders of the Romantic Range

By Johnny D. Boggs

I'm having lunch with Ol' Max Evans down in Albuquerque, and we get to talking about Western movies. Max used to cowboy, and his books explore real cowboys, most of them riding ranges in the 20th century and doing things real cowboys used to do, still do, and will continue to do. Which ain't what you see often in Hollywood movies.

Yet while Ol' Max loves the romanticism of Western movies and novels, he points out over his plate of *chile relleno*: "There's not one blankety-blank thing romantic about putting up a blankety-blank barbed wire fence!"

I'm no cowboy. I write about them, though. And I have branded calves. I've driven cattle. I've ridden through some of the most brutal country in New Mexico with two fractured ribs, thanks to a "sweet, gentle mare" named Honey who turned out to be neither sweet nor gentle but damned sure misnamed. (For the record, Honey did not buck me off. After four jumps, I bailed on my own volition when she rolled.)

Which means I get to borrow the line a stoved-up cowboy turned artist once told me: "Never been hurt, never been horseback."

At one New Mexico ranch, after my horse stumbled at a lope and sent me sailing over his head, I got to talking with a real cowboy who had recently been in a horse wreck. I showed him the big ugly bruise on my right arm. From his mouth, he removed his partial for me to inspect.

I said: "You win. Your wreck was worse than mine."

Long before Max Evans was riding the Hi Lo Country looking for strays, or cowhands were trying to save their beeves in the worst blizzards of Montana and Wyoming, or Texas waddies were pushing longhorns into Missouri and Kansas, or vaqueros were baking underneath a brutal Mexico sun, cowboys were risking their lives. It wasn't romantic. It still isn't.

It's hard work. Dangerous work.

But cowboys are iconic, not just across America, but the world. We love their independence, their hats and boots, their horses, their songs, and the imagery we've seen or read about so often thanks to Charlie Russell, William S. Hart, John Ford, Owen Wister, Will James, Max Evans, and far too many more to mention.

The cowboy is as American as baseball.

And you know what? To a city slicker or a kid or anyone who doesn't have to do it for a living, there is something truly romantic about cracking two ribs in a horse wreck or putting up a blankety-blank barbed wire fence.

Johnny D. Boggs is a six-time Spur Award-winning author based in Santa Fe, New Mexico.

Coffee's on the Fire ....

If you think the two saddest words in the English language are "afoot," you are probably a cowboy, or cowgirl. If you walk three miles to catch a horse so you can ride a mile to town, you are, again, one of those intellectual prairie fires so beloved to Western history.

And if you can see yourself even partially attached to the above paragraph, you'll probably have a bunch of fun with this book. When I finished writing the 100 items on the bucket list, I started figuring, and realized it would take four cowboys or cowgirls about six lifetimes to get all of this done, but I never claimed to be good with math. Good with horses, yes. Good with fun, oh yeah.

At this writing, I'm 72 years old, and yes, I'm a cowboy. I have done other things for a living, but I've always been a cowboy and always will be. It's an attitude. It's a chemical and psychological amalgam of blood and tissue and a jutting jaw that tells the world, hey, I'm a cowboy and if you don't like it, you can go soak your head.

But you should probably know that I have never really been a ranch cowboy. I don't know how to doctor cows, and I wouldn't know what to look for to see if they needed help. I've roped them, and I've bulldogged a number of them, I've driven them on cattle drives and branded them. Even tried riding a couple. That's when I decided that horses should be ridden and cows should be eaten.

I grew up in a suburb of Los Angeles called El Monte, and my folks had an acre of land and the riverbed of the Rio Hondo was a short block away. So when I was seven, I had a burro named Jenny whose job it was to scrape me off under an apricot tree limb. Later, when I was 14, I spent $50 I earned washing dishes to buy a horse called Two

Bits. I was a skinny kid named Tony at the time. Well, Tony and Two Bits just wasn't very intimidating to impressionable parts of the world, so we did some midstream name changing and became Slim and Tornado. The firm of Slim and Tornado had a grand time at the arenas, chasing calves around and throwing ropes at them and pretending we were the hoohaw sure-nuf combination to give nightmares to roping cattle.

Then Slim and Tornado went to the eastern High Sierra and went to work for Gene and Lona Burkhart, who owned Sequoia-Kings Pack Trains. And Slim discovered he was really a pretty good packer, a good hand at gentling young horses and a responsible guy in the backcountry with both people and stock.

This was in contrast to his "career" in rodeo, which consisted of his father referring to him as "an enthusiastic contributor of entry fees."

Embarrassing … and accurate.

So I chased wild burros in Death Valley, chased wild horses in the Coso Range, chased (in futility) after prize money in rodeos, and chased girls in college. And packed mules … always packed mules. Just wanted you to know where I'm coming from. I spent eight summers being paid to ride a horse through beautiful mountains. Didn't pay much but it sure was fun.

And those things stick with a guy for a lifetime. Since that time I've made my living as a writer, of course, but still … as a cowboy, too. Since being a cowboy is primarily an attitude, I've used this over the years to have a bunch of fun as a hunting guide in Alaska, driving a dog team in the first Iditarod Race, and generally making a nuisance of myself. And being a cowboy sure helps when it comes to sticking with a long project like writing a book.

Coffeepot on campfire. *Courtesy of Wikipedia.*

If you are a cowboy or cowgirl at heart, you're going to have some fun with this book, as I have. You realize, don't you, that we're the ones who are blessed with the companionship of horses and mules and each other? We're the ones who get to hear ... and tell ... the stories in the bunkhouses and around the campfires.

It's a great life, all in all. Live it as full out as you can. Grab opportunity with both hands and spur it into a run.

Read the book. Get some ideas. Act on them. Have a good time. Learn something and pass it on.

And save me some room at the fire, will you?

Slim Randles

SLIM RANDLES. Courtesy of Author.

The List…

100. See Horsehead Crossing

Go see the Horsehead Crossing of the Pecos. First used for cattle by Charles Goodnight and Oliver Loving when they established their trail from Texas to New Mexico in 1866, this shallow ford comes at the end of a 75-mile dry stretch for the cattle, and is one of the few places on the Pecos free of quicksand. The crossing is near Farm Road 11, about twelve miles northwest of Girvin, Texas. The historic trip by Goodnight and Loving was one of several stories that led to Larry McMurtry's story, *Lonesome Dove.* — http://en.wikipedia.org/wiki/Horsehead_Crossing

Join up with Great American Adventures for one of their unique week-long trail rides — http://great-american-adventures.com

Pecos Rodeo Grounds. Courtesy of Barbe Awalt.

99. Walk into the Prescott Rodeo Grounds

July 4, 1888, became the birthday of professional rodeo when a group of Prescott, Arizona, merchants and professional businessmen organized the first formalized "cowboy tournament" and offered cash prizes. A cowboy named Juan Leivas walked off with rodeo's first professional title and was documented in the subsequent edition of the *Arizona Journal-Miner*. — http://www.sharlot.org/library-archives/days-past/worlds-oldest-rodeo-prescott-arizona/

Bronc rider at Prescott Rodeo. Courtesy of Prescott Rodeo and Miller Photo.

98. Visit the Pendleton Round-up

The first Pendleton Round-Up was to be "a frontier exhibition of picturesque pastimes, Indian and military spectacles, cowboy racing and bronco busting for the championship of the Northwest." It turned out to be that and more.

For the initial show, all stores closed. "The largest crowd in Pendleton's history," 7,000 strong, showed up for the first show on September 29, 1910, a newspaper writer reported. Pendleton, after more than 100 years, continues to be on the short list of great professional rodeos. — http://www.pendletonroundup.com/p/About/147

PENDLETON ROUND-UP. *Courtesy of Pendleton Round-up and Elaine Cosner.*

97. Don't Miss Cheyenne Frontier Days

Cheyenne Frontier Days is an outdoor rodeo and western celebration held annually since 1897 in Cheyenne, Wyoming. The event, claimed to be one of the largest of its kind in the world, draws nearly 200,000 people every year. The celebration is held during the ten days centered about the last full week of July. In cowboy circles, it's known as "the daddy of them all." — www.cfdrodeo.com

Frontier Town at Cheyenne Frontier Days. Courtesy of Bree Anderson-Burtis, Cheyenne Frontier Days.

96. Visit Zane Grey's Cabin

Pretend you're in the real Zane Grey's cabin in Payson on the Mogollon Rim in Arizona Before you drop in at a coffee shop up there and embarrass yourself, Mogollon is pronounced MUGGY-own. You're welcome. Grey, a dentist who became one of the most famous writers of Westerns, had a pal build him a small cabin 18 miles from Payson in 1921. Then Grey lost interest in it and moved to Los Angeles. The rats and porcupines took over and the place deteriorated. A group of locals rebuilt the cabin to promote tourism, and then a forest fire burned it to the ground. So they built a close facsimile of it on Main Street in Payson and charge $5 a head to get in. Anyone in town can point the way. — www.zanegreycabin.org

FIREFIGHTERS PROTECT ZANE GREY CABIN. Courtesy of Creative Commons CC0.

95. Ride Drag on a Cattle Drive

Ride drag on a cattle drive at the Beaver Creek Guest Ranch, Alpine, Arizona. Two-day cattle drive followed by branding and vaccinations (the cows, not you) in the beautiful White Mountains of eastern Arizona. Each Fall. About $920. Call (928) 245-3083 or email info@beavercreekguestranch.com. — http://beavercreekguestranch.com/cattledrives.html

Cowboys Cattle Round Up at Jornada Experimental Range near Las Cruces, New Mexico. Courtesy of Wikipedia and sciencephoto.com.

94. Go See Mule Days in Bishop

Every Memorial Day weekend, the town of Bishop, California, on the eastern (steep) side of the High Sierra, is overrun with 30,000 visitors and a whole bunch of mules for Mule Days. Founded in 1969 by owners of nearby pack stations, including artist and poet Lona Burkhart, Mule Days has everything from races and horseshow-type events to the world's longest non-motorized parade, all to honor the world's greatest manmade animal. — http://muledays.org/

Mule Days in Bishop, CA. Courtesy of Wikipedia.

93. Visit Folsom Man Site

Visit Folsom Man Site, located about eight miles west of the small village of Folsom, New Mexico, in Wild Horse Arroyo. Why would a cowboy visit here? Well, a cowboy found the place. A black cowboy named George McJunkin was riding through the country in 1908, following an historic flood, and found bison bones uncovered by the flood. McJunkin was a self-educated student of science and realized these weren't recent bones because they were half-again as large as the bison we have today. When archaeologists later began digging, they discovered this was a kill site by ancient man, as they found spear points, known as Folsom points, between the ribs of these extinct animals. George's discovery changed history. Up to that point, man was only thought to have been in North America for 5,000 years. The Folsom find put the coming of man back to 11,000 years. — www.folsomvillage.com/folsommuseum/georgemcjunkin.html

George McJunkin. Public domain.

92. Walk On Out to Seismo's Grave

So why should a cowboy be interested in the last resting place of the world's largest dinosaur? Because it was discovered by a cowboy, of course. This approximately 150-170 foot-long lizard was found when a cowboy saw what looked like a monstrous log sticking out of a mesa near San Ysidro, New Mexico. It turned out to be part of a thigh bone that stood three stories high.

The grave is unmarked, about six miles from pavement, and then about a mile walk from the dirt road, so you'll have to ask someone in San Ysidro how to get there. Or, you can stop by the Natural History Museum in Albuquerque and watch them assemble what's left of "Seismosaurus," (Earth-shaking Lizard). — http://www.dinosaurjungle.com/dinosaur_species_seismosaurus.php

Seismosaurus. Courtesy of New Mexico Museum of Natural History and Science.

91. Head on Down to Carlsbad Caverns

Picture the Grand Canyon with a roof over it. Okay, it's not that big, but it sure seems that big. Located about 18 miles from the town of Carlsbad, New Mexico, the caverns have been a popular destination for the best part of a century. They were explored by a cowboy named Jim White, who kept telling people about them and nobody believed him for a long time. Before the caverns reached national park status, Jim built nearby White's City, which was a tourist trap for a long time.

After walking about half a day down into the earth, you come to the Big Room and walk around it to a vertical shaft called The Jumping Off Place. The ranger then tells you there are multiple caverns coming off this shaft, and one of them had been explored to a length of 18 miles and they still hadn't found the end of it. Impressive. — http://en.wikipedia.org/wiki/Carlsbad_Caverns_National_Park

Carlsbad Caverns National Park, Carlsbad, NM. Courtesy of New Mexico True.

90. Spend an Afternoon at Tejon Ranch

At nearly 270,000 acres, the historic Tejon Ranch is the largest contiguous expanse of private land in California. The property is located along Interstate 5, approximately 60 miles north of Los Angeles and 30 miles south of Bakersfield. Tejon Ranch was founded in 1843 as a Mexican land grant. In the decades that followed, the ranch grew in size as additional land grants were purchased by Tejon's founder, General Edward Fitzgerald Beale, an historic figure in early California. But what may be of most interest to cowboys is that the Tejon (ta-HONE) Ranch is the home of the old vaquero game of "once" (pronounced OWN-say), which is Spanish for eleven. When, in the old days, the vaqueros were ready to go to town and liquor up a bit, they'd have a little contest. The winner, I'm told, didn't have to buy a drink all night. These were the days of the famous California bridle horses, so each cowboy would put his pony into a full run, then slide him to a stop. They would then look to see who left the longest skid marks where the horse's hind hooves slid. The longest pair won. This was the figure eleven, of course. Or once. — http://tejonranch.com/

Tejon Ranch - View from Scissor Ridge. Courtesy of Tejon Ranch.

89. Hide Out at Hole in the Wall

The famous Hole-in-the-Wall refers to a remote defile in the Big Horn Mountains, which is today about 40 miles south of the town of Kaycee, Wyoming. In the late 19th century and the first decade of the 20th, it was the only access to a hidden basin which was a hideout for such outlaws as Butch Cassidy, Kid Curry and Blackjack Ketchum. It was nearly impossible for lawmen to approach the hideout without being detected. — http://en.wikipedia.org/wiki/Hole_in_the_Wall_Gang

Barbed Wire Fence. Courtesy of Creative Commons CC0.

88. See If You Can Find Robber's Roost

This famous hideout of the Wild Bunch isn't near anything, and experienced mountain climbers are warned to be very careful. But it is in Utah's Wayne County, and is about due east of Hanksville, Utah, and west of Canyonlands National Park. This is why Butch Cassidy chose it as a resting place between making unauthorized bank withdrawals. It is so remote that lawmen of that day never did find it. Please be careful if you go in there. — www.utah.com/oldwest/robbersroost.htm

Barbed wire. Courtesy of vsmodels.net

87. Fish Brown's Hole

Take the fly rod to Brown's Hole, Colorado. If you were to design a perfect hideout for cattle rustlers and bank robbers, it would be hard to beat Brown's Hole, known today as Brown's Park. It sits in a remote part of the Green River canyon, just a whoop and a hop from Wyoming and 35 feet from Utah. Since most posses in those days weren't allowed to cross state lines, this had an element of appeal to it.

Butch Cassidy and the Wild Bunch had cabins there, and the famous Bassett sisters lived there as well. They were not only girlfriends of the outlaws, but cattle rustlers themselves. As Ann Zwinger wrote: Brown's Hole was "a more or less permanent hideout for many who found total honesty a personal encumbrance." Brown's Hole is today a wildlife refuge and is west of Craig, Colorado, and next door to Dinosaur National Monument. I hear the fishing is good in the Green. — http://en.wikipedia.org/wiki/Browns_Park

CAMPFIRE. *Courtesy of PracticalPedal.com.*

86. Visit WS Ranch

Go visit the WS Ranch in Alma, New Mexico. This was the farthest south outlaw hideout on the Outlaw Trail. Named for the two owners, Wilson and Stevens (both wealthy Englishmen), the WS from time to time hired cowboys whose "real" names were Butch Cassidy and the Sundance Kid, (actually Robert Leroy Parker and Harry Longabaugh) but were known locally by other names. The town of Alma is gone, but the WS is still a ranch and has an interesting cemetery there.

For more information and a possible visit to the ranch, contact Apache Creek Old West Tours in nearby Reserve, New Mexico. The tours are operated by Debbie Lee, at (575) 533-6089 or apachecreekoldwesttours@gmail.com. — http://www.apachecreekoldwesttours.com

GREM LEE WITH OLIVER LEE'S SADDLE. *Courtesy of the author.*

85. Visit the Trinity Site

You can sometimes visit White Sands Missile Range in New Mexico. This is an Army base where they blow stuff up a lot and was an alternate landing field for the space shuttle. But it also has herds of the prettiest wild horses you've ever seen, and herds of African oryx.

Access to the range is only possible on the first Saturday of April and October each year; they let people drive onto the range from the north to visit the Trinity Site, where the first atomic bomb was exploded. Just keep your eyes open and look for horses and oryx. The gate to Trinity Site is about 20 miles east of I-25. Turn off at the village of San Antonio (New Mexico). The gate is well marked.

When you get a minute, go back to San Antonio and look for a huge concrete slab. That was the site of Conrad Hilton's first hotel. Across the street from the slab is a modest house with green awnings over the windows. That was his boyhood home. And the green chile cheeseburgers at the Owl Café there in San Antonio are world famous. — http://en.wikipedia.org/wiki/White_Sands_Missile_Range

Trinity Test Site New Mexico. Courtesy of Wikimedia.

84. Get Cool in the Bandera Ice Caves

Stay cool in the Bandera Ice Caves southwest of Grants, New Mexico. Worth seeing. Old lava tubes from an eruption 10,000 years ago keep water in the form of ice year-round. They're privately owned and operated mainly during the warmer months, so check first.

The late Gus Raney, who fancied himself a gunfighter and was found guilty of several murders, stored the bodies of his two teenaged boys in the ice caves before a photographer was located to take their pictures. Raney said the boys drowned in a six-inch-deep stock tank. — 1-888-ICE-CAVE, http://www.icecaves.com/

Bandera Ice Caves, Grants, NM. Courtesy of New Mexico True.

83. Be Quiet at Lucien Maxwell's Grave

Pay your respects at the grave of Lucien Maxwell, which is several miles south of the town of Fort Sumner, New Mexico, at the site of the actual fort itself. Maxwell (1818-1865) married into a huge Spanish land grant, then added to it. His holdings took in most of northeastern New Mexico and a chunk of the Texas Panhandle. He sold off a piece of the Texas portion to some wealthy cattlemen in the Panhandle and they formed the XIT Ranch. XIT stands for "Ten in Texas." That's 10 counties in Texas.

Maxwell is credited with establishing the first public school system in the territory, the first banks and the first public roads. When you're standing by Lucien's grave, you'll notice another headstone about 40 feet away inside a cage of welded rebar. It says "Pals" on it, and marks the grave of Billy the Kid and two of his buddies. You see, if you're a punk homicidal maniac, people want to steal your headstone. It's happened twice now. Maxwell was an all-right guy, so no one bothers his. — http://www.clanmaxwellusa.com/lucienb.htm

Classic New Mexico pick-up truck. Courtesy of Barbe Awalt.

82. Visit Oliver Lee State Park

Drive out to Oliver Lee State Park near Alamogordo, New Mexico. Lee once owned or controlled more than a million acres of ranchland, making him one of the all-time big cattle barons in history. He built his homestead at the mouth of Dog Canyon and became … controversial. He was a friend of Albert Fall of Teapot Dome fame and once had an ineffectual gunfight with Pat Garrett of Billy the Kid fame. His running feud with Garrett was well known, and Lee had a tunnel dug between the ranch house and an arroyo, where he always kept horses saddled in case Garrett showed up with a posse. Lee's grandson, famous Western artist Bob Lee, remembered playing in the tunnel when he was a kid.

Oliver Lee was elected to the New Mexico Senate, and was later followed in this by two grandsons. He died in 1941. One of his great-grandsons, Oliver M. "Grem" Lee IV, is a noted artist and writer and is a pard of mine. — http://www.emnrd.state.nm.us/SPD/oliverleestatepark.html

Oliver Lee State Park, Alamogordo, NM. Courtesy of New Mexico True.

81. See Kit Carson's Grave

Take off your hat for a moment at Kit Carson's grave in the Kit Carson Memorial Cemetery in Taos, New Mexico – just because you should. — www.findagrave.com/cgi-bin/fg.cgi?GRid=177&page=gr

Kit Carson Grave. Courtesy of Pinterest.com.

80. Drive by the Los Angeles Aqueduct

Two miles north of Lone Pine, California, on Highway 395, motorists can look to the west and see where erosion has washed a sizeable arroyo on the hillside. This happened just after the aqueduct was completed. The City of Los Angeles bought or condemned the entire Owens Valley, with the single exception of the George Parker Ranch near Independence. To say feelings ran high against "The City" for taking all their land and water would be an understatement. There were several attacks on the hated aqueduct, and this particular one saw night riders with dynamite "irrigating the desert" in protest. A bit of graffiti found in many restroom stalls in Inyo County – today - reads "Please flush the toilet. L.A. needs the water." — http://wsoweb.ladwp.com/Aqueduct/historyoflaa/index.htm

Los Angeles Aqueduct at Owens Valley. Courtesy of Wikimedia.

79. Visit Annie Oakley's Birthplace

About two miles northwest of Willowdell, Ohio, is a plaque marking the birthplace of one of the most legendary Western figures in history. Her name was Phoebe Ann Mosey, born in 1860. She later became famous as Annie Oakley in Buffalo Bill's Wild West Show and toured the U.S. and Europe with her trick shooting abilities. She once shot a cigarette out of Kaiser Wilhelm's mouth. It is to be noted that this was before we went to war against him. Throughout her career, it is believed that Oakley taught upwards of 15,000 women how to use a gun. Oakley believed strongly that it was crucial for women to learn how to use a gun, as not only a form of physical and mental exercise, but also to defend themselves. She said: "I would like to see every woman know how to handle guns as naturally as they know how to handle babies." She died in 1926, and her husband of 50 years, trick shooter Frank Butler, died less than three weeks later. — http://en.wikipedia.org/wiki/Annie_Oakley

Cowgirl. Courtesy of Creative Commons CC0.

78. Ride 'n Eat, Ride 'n Eat

If your name is Slim and you wish it weren't, Italian horsemen may have just the thing for you. At the four-star hotel called Resort di Scansano, a restored palatial estate in Tuscany, your one-week stay will alternate days of riding around through vineyards and olive trees with days of learning to cook from famous chefs. There is a heavy emphasis on "visiting the area's cellars" and we know what that means. If you get dirty riding around, there's a spa and an indoor pool. You'll be a pasta-making fool by the end of the week and may have to switch to a stronger horse. Peel me a grape! Eight days of this ridiculous pleasure runs $2,215. From Hidden Trails. Contact them at 1-888-9-TRAILS. — http://www.hiddentrails.com/tour/italy_scansano_relaxed_cooking.aspx

TUSCANY TRAIL RIDE. *Courtesy of Hidden Trails.*

77. Visit the Apache Kid's Graves

Mark Twain once said, "There are lies, damn lies, and statistics." In the case of the Apache Kid, a former cavalry scout who became a renegade, things got a bit out of control. For one thing, his name was Has-kay-bay-nay-ntayl. Maybe. There are two other names for him, but at least one historian claims that's just because no one knew the right way to pronounce it. He was a White Mountain Apache. He was a Pinal Apache. He was a Chiricahua Apache. He killed lots of people and never fired a shot in anger. He was active in the states of Arizona and New Mexico and in Mexico in Sonora and Chihuahua.

He was killed in 1894 and buried in some remote mountains southeast of Socorro, New Mexico. It's an official gravesite with a sign. Then he was killed again in Arizona in 1898 and was buried near Globe, Arizona. Official gravesite number two. But he died in 1933 in the Sierra Madre in Mexico and was buried in an unmarked grave. He didn't die again in New Mexico until 1935 in the Magdalena area. Official gravesite number three. This guy was tough. In fact, he was so tough that he has been sighted fairly recently, having fun in Tucson. Being a legend can be kinda fun, evidently.
— http://www.legendsofamerica.com/na-apachekid.html

Indian at Sunset. Courtesy of Creative Commons CC0.

76. Visit Charlie Russell's Studio

See Charlie Russell's studio and museum in Great Falls, Montana. It takes up an entire block, with a modern museum and gift shop as well as Russell's home and log studio. Charles Marion "Kid" Russell lived from 1864 to 1926 and started out as a working cowboy. He graduated into art by doodling for friends, drawing on napkins in exchange for drinks, and otherwise having fun. Then along came Mrs. Russell and Charlie became an industry and an institution in the West.

His paintings are the epitome of the West at that time, and they glow with life. — https://www.cmrussell.org/

Charlie Russell's Studio, Great Falls, MT. Courtesy of Wikimedia.

75. See the Frederic Remington Museum

Be sure to see the basement vaults at the Frederic Remington Museum in Ogdensburg, New York. Remington's middle name was Sackrider. I thought that was interesting, so I'm throwing it in at no extra charge. You're welcome. Remington and Russell were the artists of the West, but that's where the similarities end. Where Russell was a bunkhouse cowboy, Remington came from a wealthy family (typewriters, adding machines) in upstate New York. Remington lived from 1861 to 1909 and was quite overweight and died of appendicitis.

This museum is great, and there's a story behind it, too. When Remington died, he left behind a very beautiful widow named Eva. A wealthy guy in Ogdensburg "took her in" and cared for her until he, too, died. Then he left her the mansion where the Remington Museum is today. Yes, there was talk … according to the nice ladies at the museum. Worth a visit. — http://fredericremington.org/the-museums-c5.php

Remington Art Museum. Courtesy of Remington Art Museum.

74. Learn to Shoot from Horseback

You never know when you'll need to shoot from a running horse on your way out of town, of course. Seriously, there are several organizations that hold competitions where you shoot either a Colt .45 single-action revolver or a lever-action rifle from a running horse, while trying to hit balloons tied to stakes. You're shooting blanks, of course, and the hot embers of the black powder are enough to break the balloons at 10 to 15 feet. Two suggestions: you might want to kinda e-e-e-ease ol' Snort into this sport, and don't try this in Northfield, Minnesota. It didn't work too well there for the James and Younger bunch.

I recall loading up some deer hunters to go into the backcountry once, and one of them asked my boss, Gene Burkhart, if he could shoot off the horse he'd been assigned. Gene scratched his head and said, "Sure … once."

But if this puts the frosting on your weekend cupcake, learn more about it. You can call Mounted Shooters of America, based (where else?) in New Hampshire … (480) 243 2270, or email them at info@newmsa.com. — http://www.newmsa.com/default.aspx

Courtesy of Creative Commons CC0.

73. See Independence Rock

Ride by Independence Rock in Natrona County, Wyoming. A large, rounded rock in central Wyoming about 60 miles south of Casper on state highway 220. This was a major landmark on the Oregon, California, and Mormon Trails. It got its name because the goal of wagon trains headed for California was to reach this rock by July 4 in order to make it over the High Sierra before snow closed those passes.

It was used by countless travelers in the early 19th century as a signpost, where messages were carved in it for others who followed.

It is now part of Independence Rock State Historic Site and is accessible to the public. — http://tps.cr.nps.gov/nhl/detail.cfm?ResourceId=566&ResourceType=Site

Oregon Trail Independence Rock. Courtesy of Wikimedia.

72. Visit Lincoln County Courthouse

You might as well go to the Lincoln County Courthouse in Lincoln, New Mexico, where Billy the Kid shot and killed deputies Bell and Ollinger. You're going to, anyway. You can look out the same second-story window the way Billy did just before he shotgunned Ollinger to death.

The basement, by the way, has a ghost. It's not connected to Billy, strangely enough. Rangers there have "bumped into" a man hanging there on occasion. — http://en.wikipedia.org/wiki/Lincoln_Historic_Site

Billy the Kid. Courtesy of New Mexico True.

71. Picnic at El Morro Monument

Park for a picnic lunch at El Morro National Monument, near Ramah, New Mexico. "The Rock" is where conquistadors scratched their names and dates into the sandstone bluffs, proving that horsemen were the first Europeans to use graffiti in the United States. — www.nps.gov/elmo

El Morro National Monument, Ramah, NM. Courtesy of Wikimedia.

70. Learn About Fort Union

Touch some real history at Fort Union, near Watrous, New Mexico. This fort was established at the junction of the Cimarron Cut-Off of the Santa Fe Trail and the Mountain Route of the Santa Fe Trail. You can still see wagon ruts there today. Some wagoneers liked the Cimarron Cut-Off because it saved them time. Unfortunately, it went through the heart of Comanche territory, but at least the survivors saved time. — www.nps.gov/foun

FORT UNION NATIONAL MONUMENT, Watrous, NM. Courtesy of National Park Service.

69. Find Loma Parda

If you can, visit Loma Parda, "Sodom on the Mora." Between Watrous and Buena Vista on New Mexico 161, turn off on unmarked dirt ranch road to the right to visit the site of Loma Parda. Loma Parda was what the guys at Fort Union did for recreation before television. The activities there kept the doctor busy with various poxes and gunshot wounds.

Be sure you get permission from the ranch owner before trespassing. Unfortunately, the dance hall girls moved on many years ago. — http://el-camino-real.smugmug.com/Ghost-Towns/New-Mexico-Ghost-Towns/Loma-Parda-NM/

Western "ladies." Courtesy of Barbe Awalt.

68. Relax at the Parker Ranch

Sit in the shade at the Parker Ranch on Oak Creek near Independence, California. This is still the only ranch in the Owens Valley with its original water rights. George Parker fought the City of Los Angeles – in and out of court - and won. The ranch is an oasis of green tucked into the foothills of the Sierra a couple of miles upstream from the Mt. Whitney Fish Hatchery. — http://us.geoview.info/parker_ranch,5381247

Cowboy silhouette. Courtesy of New Mexico True.

67. Visit the Paiute Reservation Dance

Hit the Paiute Reservation Dance on Labor Day weekend, in Bishop, California. Out under the trees, by the light of small campfires, the Paiute band in Bishop celebrates Labor Day with a dance in the schoolhouse, and the stick game or "hand game" outside. Amid huffing and puffing and singing and joking around, one member of a side, or team, mixes two "sticks" (deer shin bones) one plain, one with a dark stripe. The object is for the other team to guess which hand holds the stick with the stripe. A lot of money is bet on this game, and it predates history.

A taste of history and magic under a summer night sky. — https://www.nevada150.org/sticks-and-stones-paiute-hand-games/

DANCER. Courtesy of Paiute Restoration Gathering & PowWow.

66. Take a Trail Ride in Puerto Rico

If you've always wanted to ride horses along a tropical beach, this outfit might be just the ticket for you. They operate daily out of Isabella on the northwestern coast. They accept credit cards, take good care of the horses, and want you to have fun. No prices listed, but you can always call them: (787) 872-9256 or email them: info@tropicaltrailrides.com and find out. — http://www.tropicaltrailrides.com/index.html.

Slim packing at Sawmill Meadow, CA, in 1960. Courtesy of the author.

65. Enter the Tevis Cup

The Tevis Cup is a 100-mile endurance ride from just east of Squaw Valley, California, to Auburn, California. Are you tough? Double tough? How about Ol' Snort? Can you both go over a pass in the High Sierra and down the other side, for 100 miles, in a single day?

Well, lots of other people and horses have been doing it on the Western States Trail since 1955. This is the granddaddy of endurance rides and you will learn just what the two of you are made of. Starting on the east side of the mountains, you ride over Emigrant Pass and start down the long western slope to the old gold rush town of Auburn. Much of the trail is away from roads, and volunteers help the riders and horses at a number of checkpoints. The horses are always checked for how quickly their pulse and respiration return to normal. Ol' Snort is required to have a minimum of 300 miles on him before the race, to make sure he's in shape. This is one event where Arabian horses shine, as they are pretty good endurance horses. Mustangs and Morgans have also been known to do well at these distances. For more information, call Lori Stewart at (530) 391-9101. — http://www.teviscup.org/

High mountain trail at the Tevis Cup endurance ride. Courtesy of Western States Trail Foundation and the Tevis Cup.

64. Drop into Palo Duro Canyon

You're driving across flat land for many miles and all of a sudden there's a gash in the landscape and you descend into the prettiest place in the entire Texas Panhandle. This is Palo Duro Canyon. Most of it is now a state park. A very historic place. In one of the side canyons, the cavalry shot the horses of the Quahadi Comanche and forced an end to hostilities and put them on a reservation.

But this is also the location of the JA Ranch. This was Charles Goodnight's ranch, and the JA brand was for his Scottish partner, John Adair. Goodnight was famous for his cattle trail, of course, but the fun part about the JA Ranch is Mary Ann's buffalo herd. In the old days, the JA cowboys would occasionally find an orphaned buffalo calf out on the plains and bring it back to the ranch. Mary Ann Goodnight, Charlie's wife, nursed these little guys until they were regular buffalo. Today, Mary Ann's herd numbers more than 80 head. — http://jaranch.org/

For a special treat, join up with Great American Adventures for a week-long trail ride through Palo Duro Canyon. — http://great-american-adventures.com

Palo Duro Canyon State Park, TX. Courtesy of Wikimedia.

63. Find a Seat at the National Finals Rodeo

This is the one, cowboy. The World Series and Super Bowl of rodeo. The big kahuna. The best of the best. Each fall in Las Vegas, Nevada, the top 15 professional cowboys in each event meet with the top broncs and bulls to duke it out for outrageous amounts of money and the world championships. This is held at the Thomas and Mack Center. If you can't qualify to compete there – and very few can – you can at least go and watch the best and eat at all those buffets and lose your shirt in a casino. But before you do that, better order your rodeo tickets. They range from $120 to $325 each. That's one reason they can pay more than $5.5 million in prize money. — http://www.nfr-lasvegas.com/

Unknown bulldogger, Oakdale, CA. Courtesy of the author.

62. Climb Up Pawnee Rock

Just go to the town of Pawnee Rock in Kansas and look for anything that sticks up higher than the sign on the convenience store. That's it! Just half a mile away, stand where Susan Magoffin and Kit Carson stood, looking off across the Santa Fe Trail. But they aren't there now, of course. Pawnee Rock is about 50 feet higher than the wheat field just 100 yards away, but it used to be a bunch higher. Folks who settled the area – as well as the railroad – used rock from it for construction. — http://www.legendsofkansas.com/pawneerock.html

Pawnee Rock Kansas. Courtesy of Wikimedia.

61. Visit the Pony Express Museum

Spend an hour at the Pony Express Museum, 914 Penn Street, St. Joseph, Missouri. The actual barn, in the actual place, where the Pony Express began. There's a photo of Buffalo Bill Cody standing in front of it, and it looks the same today, except now it can take longer for the post office to get a letter from St. Joseph to Sacramento. Admission $6 for adults. — http://ponyexpress.org/

Pony Express Museum, St. Joseph, MO. Courtesy of Wikimedia.

60. Hold Your Breath at the Chilcotin Mountain Race

At least watch the Mountain race on the Chilcotin Indian Reserve at Redstone, British Columbia. Starting at the top of a nearby mountain, the riders plunge their horses down a steep mountainside, ending up at the rodeo arena, some 1,500 vertical feet below. Around the third week in July each year.

Indian rodeo has really caught on in North America and there are at least three Indian Rodeo associations in the U.S. and one in Canada. They also have their own National Finals Rodeo. — http://www.straight.com/article/chilcotin-rodeo-racers-live-on-skill-and-nerve-0

Chilcotin Mountain Race, Redstone, BC. Courtesy of Wikimedia.

59. Visit Quanah Parker Star House

Check out the Quanah Parker Star House, Cache, Oklahoma. Parker (1845 to 1911) was the last chief of the Comanche people following their defeat and removal to Fort Sill Reservation. He built a huge house with the financial help of the owner of the 6666 Ranch, Samuel Burk Burnett, and was instrumental in forming the Native American Church. He became quite a wealthy cattleman, which was a good thing because he was married to Weakeah and Chony and Mah-Chetta-Wookey and Ah-Uh-Wuth-Takum and Coby and Toe-Pay and Tonarcy. They needed the money. — http://en.wikipedia.org/wiki/Quanah_Parker_Star_House

Quanah Parker Star House, Cache, OK. Courtesy of Wikipedia.

58. Learn Backcountry First Aid

Learn backcountry first aid for your horse. Ol' Snort will thank you for keeping him in good shape. One way to learn this, short of going off to vet school for 100 years, is to put together a horse first-aid kit and learn how to use it. The Squaw Butte Chapter of the Backcountry Horsemen of Idaho has assembled all this into an easily learned study. It's free, just go read it and put your own first aid outfit together. It sure beats walking home. — http://www.bchi.org/education-manual/Equine%20First%20Aid.pdf

Slim & Tornado heading for the mountains about 1958. Courtesy of the author.

57. Visit the National Cowboy Hall of Fame

Earn your own spot at the National Cowboy Hall of Fame, which changed its name. It's now The National Cowboy & Western Heritage Museum, 1700 NE 63rd Street in Oklahoma City, Oklahoma. While you're there, ask them why they changed the name. Can you say "donations?" I knew you could.

Of course, if you're already IN the Hall of Fame, cowboy, congratulations! — en.wikipedia.org/wiki/Cowboy_Hall_of_Fame

The End of the Trail. Courtesy of National Cowboy & Western Heritage Museum.

56. See the Pro Rodeo Hall of Fame

Don't look for my picture at the Pro Rodeo Hall of Fame, 101 Pro Rodeo Dr., Colorado Springs, Colorado. This is more than a building full of memories of the greatest in rodeo's history. It's an organization that sponsors events and scholarships and all kinds of interesting things. I'm especially interested in what they call a "spirited mixer." You know what we used to call it. Open seven days a week. — http://www.prorodeohalloffame.com/

Rodeo. Courtesy of Bree Anderson-Burtis, Cheyenne Frontier Days.

55. Get Inspired at Badger Clark's Cabin

It's called "Badger Hole," of course, and was the home of the famous poet of the West for the last 30 years of his life. Charles "Badger" Clark was the first poet laureate of South Dakota, and his home is open to the public. The Badger Hole is located south of U.S. Highway 16A on the Badger Clark Road, inside Custer State Park. — http://gfp.sd.gov/state-parks/directory/custer/sights/badger-hole.aspx

Wall of skulls. Courtesy of New Mexico True.

54. See J. Frank Dobie's House

Dobie, one of the best chroniclers of the early days of Texas, bought the house at 702 E. Dean Keeton, in Austin, Texas, in 1926, and lived in it (and wrote in it) until his death in 1964. The University of Texas bought the house and it is now used by the Michener Center for Writers. Dobie's best-known work was probably *The Longhorns*. — http://en.wikipedia.org/wiki/J._Frank_Dobie

J. Frank Dobie House in Austin, Tx. Courtesy of Wikipedia.

53. Check Out the Haley Library

J. Evetts Haley (1901-1995) was a noted historian and sometimes controversial political pundit in Texas. A former cowboy and lifelong rancher, he sought an education and got it, both formally and informally throughout his long life. His most famous work is a biography of Charles Goodnight, the cattleman, who with Oliver Loving, founded the Goodnight-Loving Trail to New Mexico. Haley's library was set up by him and by his wife, Nita Stewart Haley, as a free-of-charge research library at 1805 West Indiana Ave. in Midland, Texas. — http://www.haleylibrary.com/; http://en.wikipedia.org/wiki/J._Evetts_Haley

Cattle Drive. Courtesy of Bree Anderson-Burtis, Cheyenne Frontier Days.

52. Visit Kemper Campbell Ranch

Say hi to the Red House for me at the Kemper Campbell Ranch in Victorville, California (I used to live there). This is a former guest ranch on the Mojave River, just over a small hill and walking distance from downtown Victorville. Movie stars stayed there for many years while on location. One of its guests was cowboy writer/artist Will James. He stayed there while helping on a motion picture in 1942. He used to walk over the hill every evening and line his insides with liquid refreshment at a bar, and the bar is still there and still open. He'd use soap to draw beautiful pictures of the West on the mirror behind the bar, and the bartender would wash them off the next day. One night, Will drew a picture of a bucking horse on the mirror, then walked back to the Kemper Campbell Ranch and died. The bartender got word of his death ten minutes after he'd finished cleaning the mirror. — http://mojavehistory.com/interview-campbelldeblasis.html

Old Pick-up. Courtesy of New Mexico True.

51. Sleuth Out the Mysterious Kansas Bull Roping

Ranchers in a sparsely populated area of the Flint Hills have found a way to combine work and competition. When yearling bulls have been selected to become steers, instead of just running them through a squeeze chute or team roping them, local hands have a timed contest. According to a former participant, the cowboy goes out and ropes a bull, "fairgrounds" him by throwing the rope around his butt as he rides by, and dumping him. He then goes down to the bull, pulls out his knife, and "harvests" Rocky Mountain oysters. The flag is dropped and the time stopped when the contestant holds both "trophies" in the air.

This isn't well known, of course, as this method of roping is illegal in Kansas, as well as in most other states. But hey, when you live in a town of less than 100 people, and the only bar in the place has closed down ....

So we're not revealing the name of the town.

CUTTING. *Courtesy of pixta.com/patrimonio.*

50. Eat a Rocky Mountain Oyster

As a worthy follow-up to number 51, be sure to dine on bull testicles before you sign out. These are usually (always) available after a branding, and there are several ways of fixing them. One pard of mine says he just shushes them around in the water trough and puts them on top of a hot branding iron until they're cooked on both sides. One popular cooking scheme is to roll them in beaten eggs and cracker crumbs and then fry them. Another way is to cook them, grind them up, and mix them with scrambled eggs. Give it a try, cowboy, you'll have a ball!

Here are some more ideas: https://search.yahoo.com/yhs/search?p=rocky+mountain+oysters&ei=UTF-8&hspart=mozilla&hsimp=yhs-001

Rocky Mountain Oysters. Courtesy of Wikimedia.

49. Dine at Luna Mansion in Los Lunas

Solomon Luna was a prominent sheep rancher in this community about 10 miles south of Albuquerque. Born in 1858, Luna was courted heavily by the railroad, which wanted an easement through his ranch. He said no. So the railroad treated Luna and Mrs. Luna to a grand tour around the country on the train. Solomon really liked the Southern mansions, so he told the railroad they could run the train through his place if they built him a mansion just like those ... except, of course, it had to be built of adobe. They did. Today it's a restaurant.

Solomon Luna died in 1912 when he fell into a vat of sheep dip and drowned. — http://lunamansion.com/

Luna Mansion, Los Lunas, NM. Courtesy of Barbe Awalt.

48. Tip Your Hat to Colorado Springs

Yep. The whole town. The entire town, you see, is a monument to a remarkable man. William Jackson Palmer was born in 1836, and despite being a Quaker, became a general in the Civil War. His cavalry captured Confederate President Jefferson Davis, and did so much traveling by night they were known as "Palmer's Owls." Palmer was a recipient of the Medal of Honor.

After the war, General Palmer took up his old trade as a builder of railroads. He was in Pueblo, Colorado, one day, and his top engineers explained to him for six hours why it was impossible to build a railroad to the gold mines deep in the Rocky Mountains. He listened quietly, then said, "We start in the morning." The result was the Denver and Rio Grande Railroad. He later built the Mexican National Railway. He also founded Durango and Alamosa, Colorado.

Palmer built Colorado Springs as a community for affluent families from Back East. He laid out the streets and designed the whole place, and if you wanted to build a home there, you signed a piece of paper saying if you got drunk, you lost your property. — http://en.wikipedia.org/wiki/William_Jackson_Palmer

Cowboy hats. Courtesy of GraphicStock.com.

47. Browse the Rhodes Collection

Browse the Eugene Manlove Rhodes Collection at the public library in Alamogordo, New Mexico. A library collection? Instead of a visit to the grave or the ranch of a noted "cowboy chronicler" and cowboy himself? Well, yes. Because Gene Rhodes's grave, and his ranch house, are in the San Andres Mountains in the middle of the White Sands Missile Range, and there are some very earnest 19-year-old soldiers with M16s who won't let you go there. Rhodes (1869 to 1934) was a friend to all during his cowboy and ranching days, and this sometimes became a problem. Among his visitors were outlaws Bill Doolin and Sam Ketchum. One of Rhodes' houseguests killed a deputy sheriff in a gunfight in Rhodes' horse corral. And Rhodes was occasionally at odds with Pat Garrett over his indiscriminate hospitality.

About the only way to visit his old digs legally would be to get drawn in the once-in-a-lifetime oryx hunt specifically in that area. Well, you could … no, not that, either. I guess the only way to visit Rhodes's grave is to be born there.

His headstone says "Pasó por aqui" (he passed by here), which was the title of his most famous short story. — http://rhodesfamily.org/eugene_manlove_rhodes.php

White Sands National Monument. Courtesy of New Mexico True.

46. See the Will Rogers Monument

Wear a parka while visiting Will Rogers Monument. Trick roper and humorist Will Rogers was killed in 1935, along with the famous aviator Wiley Post, when their plane lost power shortly after takeoff and crashed into a lagoon. Two monuments were erected at the site, which is 13 miles southwest of the village of Barrow, Alaska, the northernmost community in the United States. To find the markers, go to the north side of Walakpa Bay, near the mouth of the Walakpa River. — http://en.wikipedia.org/wiki/Rogers-Post_Site

Will Rogers Monument, Barrow, AK. Courtesy of Geocaching.com.

45. Pay Your Respects to Sacagawea's Monuments

Three of them. Visit all three, as she was a remarkable woman. After serving as guide and interpreter for the Lewis and Clark expedition of 1804-1805, she either died at the age of 24 or lived to be 98 years old. A statue of her stands at the state capitol in Bismarck, North Dakota, and a nice headstone was placed in the cemetery in Fort Washakie, Wyoming, where many believed she had lived to a very old age. And there's a third statue as well, at the National Cowgirl Hall of Fame in Fort Worth, Texas. She was inducted posthumously in 1977. She was of the Lemhi Shoshone tribe which lived near present-day Salmon, Idaho. — http://en.wikipedia.org/wiki/Sacagawea

SACAGAWEA. *Courtesy of Wikipedia.*

44. See Slaughter Mesa

Ask directions to Slaughter Mesa near Apache Creek, New Mexico. Named for cattleman and lawman Texas John Slaughter, Slaughter Mesa is perhaps best known today as one of the top places to hunt trophy elk in the state. Slaughter divided his time between this area and southern Arizona. His cowboys were involved in the famous Elfego Baca shootout in nearby Reserve, New Mexico. — http://en.wikipedia.org/wiki/John_Horton_Slaughter

Bull Elk. Courtesy of Creative Commons CC0.

43. Visit Story Mansion

Take some time to see the Story Mansion in Bozeman, Montana. Most of us are at least partly familiar with the story of Nelson Story, Sr., 1838 to 1936, who drove the first large herd of cattle from Texas to Montana at the close of the Civil War. That's because his exploits were partially responsible for inspiring Larry McMurtry to write *Lonesome Dove*. Story had struck a rich gold claim in 1863 in Alder Gulch, Montana, then went to Texas and bought 3,000 head of cattle and started them north.

Along the way, he argued with the cavalry, fought the Sioux and Crow (losing one cowboy in the process), and finally got the herd to Montana, where he provided beef for the miners. It was four years before anyone else made another cattle drive to Montana. His shrewd business sense made him a fortune and established him as one of the founders of the cattle industry in the state. — http://www.bozeman.net/Departments-(1)/Park--Rec-Cemetery/Recreation/Facilities/Story

RIDE 'EM COWBOY. *Courtesy of Jackie Cercek.*

42. Tip Your Hat at York's Statue

York was the only African-American on the Lewis and Clark Expedition, and he was Captain William Clark's personal slave. During this two-year expedition, he saved Lewis's life once and Clark's life once. He experienced quite a bit of freedom during the long trip and was treated as any other member of the expedition. Back in civilization, York requested his freedom and Clark later said it was granted. York's years after that aren't clear. Some say he died in 1822 in Kentucky, but another source said York was seen living with the Sioux as late as 1834, that he had four wives, and was fluent in their language.

A statue to this explorer stands in the Riverfront Plaza/ Belvedere in Louisville, Kentucky. — http://en.wikipedia.org/wiki/York_%28explorer%29

Cowboy hat. Courtesy of GraphicStock.com.

41. Drop In at McGowan Saddlery

Terrance & Kate McGowan make Vaquero balanced-ride saddles at 4511 Alcorn Road in Fallon, Nevada. The saddle should fit the horse as well as the rider. — www.mcgowansaddlery.com

SADDLE. *Diamond Back, by Rick Bean, TCAA (Photo by Carla C. Cain) Courtesy of National Cowboy & Western Heritage Museum.*

40. Take in the Cowboy Poetry Gathering

Tune up your doggerel (and catterel) for the Cowboy Poetry Gathering, each February in Elko, Nevada.

If you can't get enough of guys rhyming while wearing spurs indoors and sporting great handlebar moustaches, this will get your tank topped off. — http://www.westernfolklife.org/General-Information-on-the-Gathering/national-cowboy-poetry-gathering-home-page.html

THE ALAMO. *Courtesy of Barbe Awalt.*

39. Buy Something at J.M. Capriola Co.

Drop in at the J.M. Capriola Co., located at 500 Commercial Street, in Elko, Nevada. The store with the red horse on the roof. A walk back in time, and the home place, the *querencia*, of Garcia Bits and Spurs. You'll wish you were wealthy. — http://capriolas.com/

Boots on the bumper. Courtesy of New Mexico True.

38. Visit Jordan Valley Big Loop Rodeo

In the Spring of the year, go see the Jordan Valley Big Loop Rodeo in Jordan Valley, Oregon.

This is a different kind of rodeo. Events include team roping wild horses, and saddle bronc riding with a regular stock saddle, including having a catch rope tied to the saddle strings. And the ride is 10 seconds, not eight, the way it was back in the 50s.

Bring a tent and camp out. Bring your horses, dogs and kids. This is a small cowboy town, so good luck on hot showers. The rodeo arena is directly across the street from the cemetery. Coincidence? Hey, why drive farther than you have to? — http://www.bigloopro deo.com

"Give him a ten" at Big Loop Rodeo. Courtesy of Jackie Cercek.

37. Talk to the Folks at Colorado Saddlery

For more than 60 years, Colorado Saddlery in Golden has made saddles for working cowboys and working horses and mules. These are saddles that will last several lifetimes, but be prepared to spend a bit more than two grand for one. — https://www.coloradosaddlery.net/

Wall of skulls. Courtesy of New Mexico True.

36. Take a Horseback Tour of Mongolia

Sign up with Leo Murray – an American living in Hong Kong – for a horseback expedition into remotest Mongolia. Leo puts one of these expeditions together every summer, sometimes using camels for pack animals, sometimes oxen.

A friend of the author has gone several times and loves it. Wild country. Friendly people.

About 20 days. About $7,000. Leo uses www.nomads-tours.com for his trips. You may reach him at hkmurray@hkstar.com.

Mongolian horseback expedition. Courtesy of Amy Marash.

35. Get a GOOD Cowboy Hat

Slim Randles and his favorite hat. Courtesy of author.

No cowboy is complete without a "lid," but there are cowboy hats and cowboy hats. There are some universal truths about a good hat: 1. The only way to break one in is to wear it … a lot; 2. Straw hats (Panama hats – actually made in Ecuador) are only for summer; 3. Fur felt hats are for always and forever.

A guide to choosing the "right" fur felt hat is simply this: get the hat with the most X's you can afford. These hats are made of beaver fur blended with wool. The number of X's indicates the amount of fur in the hat. A 5X hat is acceptable to most working cowboys. Anything less than that is for hangers-on in Santa Fe bars or a Tucson pimp or square dance callers.

A 10X beaver hat is excellent, and a 15X beaver is so well made your heirs can use it after you kick the … well, you know.

Every one of those X's will cost you plenty. If you spend less than $100 for a fur felt hat, you either are dancing on the edges of a screaming deal, or you probably don't want it.

A good hat is forever. Old Grant Dalton and I packed mules together. His dad was one of the family members who were gunned down in Coffeyville, Kansas, after making an unauthorized withdrawal from a local bank. Grant never took off his hat. Slept with it. I wasn't around when he died, but eyewitnesses reported that he was actually bald. Who knew?

And if you really want to get fancy with a bucket list hat, and money is no object, check into Montecristi Custom Hats in Santa Fe, New Mexico. Look them up at http://www.montecristihats.com/ and you can see they'll let you spend as much as $5,000 on a cowboy hat.

And if you should break in your new hat by having a horse step on it, which isn't recommended, remember to remove your head from it first.

OLD GRANT DALTON PACKING ON SHEPHERD'S PASS. *Courtesy of the author.*

34. Go to Calf Roping School

Take your piggin' string to Calf Roping School. To learn how to be a good tie-down calf roper, learn from the best. Consider attending a roping school taught by eight times world champion Joe Beaver. And private roping lessons are also available. This isn't just for kids, either. Want to advance to the next level? Call Joe (979) 777-6946, or email him at info@joebeaver.com. His schools are held all over the country. — http://www.joebeaver.com/schoolschamps.html

Roping. *Courtesy of sithtech.net.*

33. Learn at Team Roping School

Dally up at Team Roping School. Allow me a personal note here. It's my first junior rodeo, I'm 14, and I'm in the calf roping in Hemet, California. I noticed two younger kids, both riding overgrown what-looked-like brown ponies. Didn't pay much attention to them. Wasn't I the he-man freshman in high school from the tall lonelies … aka a suburb of Los Angeles? Well, those two brothers killed us. Dead. They were Leo and Jerold Camarillo, and those were names lots of us weren't likely to forget. World champions, both of them. And they both teach team roping today, the safest and most popular of all rodeo events (because kids and old guys can do it, too). But just because it's the safest rodeo event, keep in mind that Reagan's Secretary of Commerce, Malcolm Baldridge, was killed while team roping. Call Jerold at (209) 606-8482 or Leo at (928) 636-4731.

And when you see them, tell them the only reason they beat me in 1956 was 1. Superior talent, 2. Great horses, 3. A father who coached them, 4. Athletic ability, 5. Daily practice, and 6. the sun was in my eyes. If it weren't for those …..! — http://camarilloteamroping.com/schools_lessons.htm.

Leo and Jerold Camarillo at age 10 and 12. Courtesy of the author.

32. Sign Up for Bronc Riding School

Go to Saddle Bronc Riding School. You can learn from one of the best, Lyle Sankey. And you can learn at one of his many traveling clinics, or at his home arena in Kansas. It's $415 for a three-day clinic on the road for bronc riders age 14 through adult, and $440 for the four-day clinic in Kansas. Call Lyle at (417-263-7777. — http://www.shop.sankeyrodeo.com/Rodeo-schools_c4.htm

RODEO BRONC RIDER. Courtesy of Bree Anderson-Burtis, Cheyenne Frontier Days.

31. Be a Head Cruncher

Take time to be a head cruncher ... attend steer wrestling school. 2001 world champion Rope Myers hosts a steer wrestling school in Van, Texas, and if sliding off the back of a perfectly good horse onto some horns bobbing up and down at 30 miles an hour sounds like fun, go for it! His school costs $300 for a weekend, and you can rent a good doggin' horse for $75 from him. Or you can buy a steer-saver mechanical steer for $1,675 plus shipping. Saves on feed, too.

Little-known fact: I personally hold the record for the slowest time for a 135-pound cowboy in professional steer wrestling at the annual rodeo in Lone Pine, California. Sixty-three seconds flat! I recall looking up at the flag man after finally getting the steer down and asked what he thought my time was. His reply ... "Well, it's still Saturday." — http://ropemyers.com/schools/

Rodeo Steer Wrestling. Courtesy of Wikipedia.

30. Go Say Hello to Bill Pickett

Go say hello to Bill Pickett. If you went to doggin' school and liked it, go visit Bill Pickett's grave. Pickett, who stood 5'7" and weighed 145 lbs., invented bulldogging, which was later renamed steer wrestling after the Politically Correct Police came along. He is buried in the shadow of the White Eagle Monument in the cemetery in Marland, Oklahoma. He lived from 1870 to1932, and Colonel Zach Miller of the 101 Wild West Show called Pickett "the greatest sweat and dirt cowboy who ever lived." Bill was fatally injured when he fell under a horse and was kicked in the head. He is a member of both the National Cowboy Hall of Fame and the Rodeo Hall of Fame, and the Bill Pickett Invitational Rodeo in Los Angeles was named for him. The rodeo features black cowboys. Pickett was the first black cowboy to have a movie made about his exploits.

Times have really changed since Pickett's time. Today, there are at least seven rodeo associations, regional and national, for black cowboys, along with the National Black Rodeo Finals which is held each year in Bossier City, Louisiana. — http://www.findagrave.com/cgi-bin/fg.cgi?page=gr&GRid=811

101 Wild West Show. Courtesy of Wikipedia.

29. Try Barrel Racing School

Take your turn at Barrel Racing School. If you want to be the best barrel racer in the world, you need to learn from the best, and that would be Charmayne James, a native of Clayton, New Mexico, who won her first world championship at 14 years old, and then won ten more in a row. This means she owned two world championship brand-new pickup trucks before she was old enough to drive! She's the only woman to win more than a million dollars in the event, and she gives barrel racing clinics all over the country. For more, call (830) 755-8888 or email clinics@charmaynejames.com. An interesting side note here: Charmayne's most famous barrel horse was a gelding named Scamper. He once won a go-round in barrel racing at the National Finals Rodeo after his bridle fell off. He died in 2012, and of course, since he was a gelding, couldn't father any babies. Naturally, that kind of equine talent shouldn't be allowed to just die out, so Charmayne had him cloned while he was still with us. The clone is named "Clayton" and was left a stud and is standing. Since clones aren't recognized for registration in the Quarter horse books, you can't register the foal, but you'll get a high-tech biological son or daughter of Scamper, anyway. — http://charmaynejames.com/

Barrel Racing. Courtesy of Bree Anderson-Burtis, Cheyenne Frontier Days.

28. Take Cutting Horse Lessons

You should both take Cutting Horse Lessons. If riding a horse that knows a lot more than you do appeals to you, take cutting lessons. You can ride your own Snort into a corral and make a ducker and dodger out of him, or you can inherit General Foods and go buy one already trained.

Leon Harrel is something of a legend in the world of cutting horses, having won five world championships, and his clinics are highly rated. In cutting, both the horse and the rider need to be trained, so don't just send Snort off for lessons.

Give Leon a call for more information at (817)-523-5221. — http://www.leonharrel.com/index.htm

Cutting. Courtesy of pixta.com/patrimonio.

27. Learn Packing School Fundamentals

Go to packing school. If you want to learn the right way to take Ol' Snort into the high country for a vacation, or if packing for a living appeals to you (I did it for eight summers and it's fantastic … it gives you everything you need except sleep), you can go up to Rock Creek Pack Station north of Bishop, California, on the eastern side of the High Sierra, and learn the right and safe way to do it. You can email them at info@rockcreekpackstation.com. A course in the fundamentals costs around $1,000. Be sure you learn how to tie the High Sierra Hooligan while you're there. It's fast. I've won the packing contest at the New Mexico State Fair using that hitch. — http://www.rockcreekpackstation.com/pack_school.shtml

Rock Creek Pack Station Pack Trip. Courtesy of Rock Creek Pack Station.

26. Take a "Selfie" with Elfego Baca

Take a "selfie" at Elfego Baca Monument in Reserve, New Mexico. Elfego Baca was a legendary figure during his lifetime, and having a Disney movie made about your life didn't hurt, either. This young deputy sheriff was in the village of Middle Frisco Plaza (now Reserve) in October of 1884 and arrested a young cowboy there. The arrestee was one of Texas John Slaughter's hands. The rest of the Slaughter outfit didn't take kindly to the arrest and went after the deputy. Baca holed up in a jacal (mud and stick shack). After Baca killed Slaughter's foreman, the cowboys (somewhere between 40 and 80 of them) poured gunfire into the shack for 30 hours. Baca was untouched, although 4,000 rounds were fired at him, and he managed to kill four and wound eight of his attackers.

Baca in later years was not only sheriff of Socorro County, but was a lawyer in Socorro, El Paso and Albuquerque. His legend extended even into the courtroom. There's one story of a client wiring him in Albuquerque from El Paso asking him to come immediately, as he'd been charged with murder. Baca wired back: "Leaving immediately with three eyewitnesses." — http://en.wikipedia.org/wiki/Elfego_Baca

Selfie stick. *Courtesy of SelfieStichCentral.com.*

25. Sit Up Straight at Spanish Riding School

Wear a necktie at the Spanish Riding School. The world-famous Spanish Riding School in Vienna, Austria, will be 450 years old in 2015. The horses and most of the instructors are younger than that. So if you ever wanted to wear one of those Napoleon hats and make a white horse jump off the ground, here's your chance. You can take a riding clinic for 90 euros, or go watch them do this ancient equestrian dance for a lot less than that.

Of course, being a cowboy, you might think 90 euros is a lot of money to pay to have a horse jump off the ground with you. You can always pay less than that for entry fees in the saddle bronc riding and have a similar experience, but those Lipizzaner stallions are a lot smoother. — http://www.srs.at/en/tradition/the-spanish-riding-school/

LIPIZZANER STALLIONS.. *Courtesy of flikr.com..*

24. Visit Meriwether Lewis' Grave

Take a few minutes at Meriwether Lewis's grave. The famous explorer suffered from mental problems and died from what was probably self-inflicted gunshot wounds at an inn called Grinder's Stand, on October 11, 1809. He had been on his way to Washington D.C. at the time. Lewis was buried in the yard of the inn, which is now a national monument in his honor, and is about seven miles east of what is now Hohenwald, Tennessee. At the time of his death he was governor of Louisiana Territory, appointed by his close friend, Thomas Jefferson. He was 35 years old. — http://en.wikipedia.org/wiki/Meriwether_Lewis

Meriwether Lewis grave. Courtesy of Wikimedia.

23. Bag It at Buffalo Bill Museum

Take your sleeping bag to the Buffalo Bill Museum in Cody, Wyoming. Well, actually, it's a much bigger deal than that, because it's now the Buffalo Bill Center of the West and has five museums and a research library. The fabled cavalry scout, buffalo hunter and showman has his museum there, but the place also includes the Draper Natural History Museum, the Whitney Western Art Museum, the Plains Indian Museum, the Cody Firearms Museum and the McCracken Research Library.

I'm told you can't see it all in one day, and it costs nineteen bucks a head to get in. — http://centerofthewest.org/explore/buffalo-bill/

BUFFALO BILL'S WEST WEST SHOW POSTER, CA. 1899. COURTESY OF WIKIPEDIA.

22. See Max Evans' Birthplace

Do a drive-by at Max Evans' birthplace when you're attending the National Cowboy Symposium. Ol' Max, the dean of writers about the West, was born in a house in the country which is now a house in the town of Ropes, Texas, about 20 miles south of Lubbock. This was in 1924, and the town, which was founded by his grandfather, a local merchant, grew out to meet the house. There is no house number on it, but it's on the southeast corner of Roundup and Timmons, and is, according to Max, "Pale blue with a big ol' hole in the roof." Max's younger brother died in infancy and was buried in the backyard. Evans, a self-taught painter as well as a self-taught writer, is best known for *The Rounders*, but also contributed some giant pieces of literature like *Bluefeather Fellini*, and *The Hi Lo Country*.

For more information on Max Evans, I can suggest reading *Ol' Max Evans, the First Thousand Years* ... which I wrote. — http://www.amazon.com/Ol-Max-Evans-First-Thousand/dp/0826335896

Max Evans filming The Ballad of Cable Hogue, *1970, Echo Bay, Nevada. Courtesy of Pat Evans.*

21. Visit the Kodiak Rodeo

They don't rope moose at the Kodiak Rodeo. The city of Kodiak, on Kodiak Island, Alaska, has had a rodeo in late summer for more than 40 years. There are cattle ranches on the island, and the bull riding is generally done on range bulls. They have plenty of cattle for the roping events, but broncs are another thing entirely. They had to "flank out" regular riding horses to get some bucking action. I attended one of the earliest rodeos there, and watched a man win the calf roping and the saddle bronc riding … on the same horse. — http://www.discoverourtown.com/AK/Kodiak/Events/kodiak-rodeo-state-fair/312260.html

BRONC RIDING. Courtesy of Wikimedia.

20. Enjoy the National Cowboy Symposium

Wear a bolo tie at the National Cowboy Symposium in mid-September in Lubbock, Texas. If you like anything to do with cowboys and ranch life … show up and have fun. There are panels of cowboy artists, panels of cowboy writers, panels of cowboy poets, panels of cowboy singers, and not a single panel truck in sight.

Lots of fun. Grow a big moustache, wear your jeans inside your boots, and wear spurs (with jinglebobs) in the building. They'll think you're about to spout a poem about the day the cat fell into the water trough. Learn more! (806) 798-7825. — http://www.cowboy.org/

Cowboy Symposium camp site. *Courtesy of New Mexico True.*

19. Braid Some Rawhide

If you're like I am and find the feel and look of braided rawhide stirs some memory deep inside, learn how to do it yourself. Traditional Cowboy Arts Association has a number of suggestions on how to learn this ancient craft, but why not learn from one of the greatest rawhide artists in the world? Leland Hensley, in Texas, gives occasional workshops around the country, and his work is as good as it comes. To learn about the next clinic, call Leland at (254) 717-7335 or email him at braider@lelandhensley.com. — http://www.lelandhensley.com/

Leland Henlsey Ladies Braided Bolo Tie. Courtesy of NCWHM.

18. Go to Farrier School

And learn the right way to "git arn on 'em." One noted school is the Oklahoma Horseshoeing School in Purcell, Oklahoma. They shoe live horses all day, every day, and start a new small group of students each Monday.

The courses range from two weeks ($1,650) to 12 weeks ($6,200). The graduates include full-time professional farriers who do corrective shoeing and advanced blacksmithing to part-time farriers who do other things as an occupation. Call (405) 288-6085 or email OkHorseschool@aol.com, and someday you, too, will be able to say, "Oh, my aching back!" — http://www.horseshoes.net/basic.php To learn about the farrier industry and schools in your area, check out www.americanfarriers.org.

Horseshoe. Courtesy of Creative Commons CC0.

17. Visit the Santa Ynez Museum

Try the Santa Ynez Valley Historical Museum in Santa Barbara County, California. Try to be there for the Vaquero Show and Sale in November. This is the land of the hackamore, the spade bit, the plaited rawhide reins, the reined horse and the birthplace of dally roping. The museum features things from the vaquero days of California year-round, and during the show and sale, you can see experts at the ancient skills making these things today. — http://www.seecalifornia.com/events/santa-ynez-vaquero-show.html

Cowboy Museum, Santa Ynez, CA. Courtesy of Pinterest, photo by Deby "Jones" O'Gorman.

16. Make Spurs and Bits

If you've always wanted to take some steel and create something beautiful out of it – for cowboys – you might want to consider heading to Canada and learn the right way to do it from Vernon and Susan Lynes. Their four-week course costs $3,000 and includes room and board. You will be expected to make at least four items during your course and will be issued a certificate upon completion. The Lynes live in Bonnyville, Alberta. Call them at (780) 826-2047 or email them at info@lynescustomcowboyco.com. — http://www.lynescustomcowboyco.com/courses/

Spurs. Courtesy of Creative Commons CC0..

15. Make Your Own Saddle

You can pay two grand or more for a saddle which may or may not fit you and your horse, or you can spend $4,800 for a four-week course and learn how to build your own. Pete Harry in Kentucky teaches just such a course, and it may be a steppingstone to your new career. For no additional money, Pete will tell you what it means to skive. Call Pete at (270) 886-5448 or email him at petescustomsaddles@gmail.com. — http://petescustomsaddles.com/school.html

Tooled Saddle. Courtesy of Wikipedia.

14. Make Your Own Hatband

From a snakeskin. Obviously, since you're a macho guy, you'll want it to be a rattlesnake skin. Here's how I did it. Skin snake. Remove as much flesh as possible from the inside of the skin. Roll the skin and put it in a glass jar filled with a mixture of ½ glycerin and ½ rubbing alcohol. Make sure the solution reaches all parts of the skin. Stir the mixture each day with a stick or wooden spoon. After three days, remove the skin, scrape off any remaining meat on the underside, and work pure glycerin into it with your fingers. Lay it out, flesh side up, and let it work overnight. Then rinse the skin thoroughly with lukewarm water and let it hang and dry in a dark place for 24 hours. This will give you a hatband that is as soft and supple as roping gloves.

One word of caution here: Be certain you remove the snake from the skin before you begin. And cut the head off and bury it first thing. Yes, a dead snake CAN kill you. —http://www.thetanneryinc.com/snakeskin.html

Rattlesnake. Courtesy of Creative Commons CC0.

13. Look at Ladies' Day

It's always Ladies' Day at The National Cowgirl Hall of Fame. Located in the Fort Worth Museum of Science and History at 1600 Gendy St. in Fort Worth, Texas, the hall of fame honors outstanding cowgirls of modern day and of history. It costs $15 a head for adults.

While you're there, look for a picture of Mabel Strickland. Mabel (1897-1976) outrode and outroped most men in the early days of rodeo, and then went to work in Hollywood as an actress and stunt rider, in one film doing the stunt riding for Bing Crosby. Mabel won the bronc riding and the women's all-around championship at Cheyenne Frontier Days in 1922, and also won at Pendleton and Madison Square Garden. So smile at her picture and say hi to a great champion.

Before you leave the hall of fame, be sure to tip your hat to Lucille Mulhall's exhibit. One of the very first cowgirls to break on the scene, Lucille (1885-1940) rode broncs and was one of the few women to ever compete in single steer roping. Later, she rode in the 101 Wild West Show and then started her own. She was killed in a car accident in 1940, just a mile from her home in Mulhall, Oklahoma. — http://www.fwmuseum.org/national-cowgirl-museum-and-hall-fame-1

Cowgirl BBQ, Santa Fe, NM. Courtesy of Barbe Awalt.

12. Own at Least One Gun ... Safely

Every cowboy should have at least one decent gun in his lifetime. Why? Well … *because.* So, assuming you know how to handle one safely (and if you don't … learn first) here are my suggestions.

Old-time ranch cowboys almost always had a side-arm with them in the saddlebags. Why? Because a bucking horse can cost you a lost gun somewhere out in the brush when you finally pick yourself up and notice an empty holster. Today, however, we have holsters that will fit just about any kind of handgun you can name, and will hold onto it even during a bucking spell.

Old-time cowboys carried one with them for snakes or in case some injured animal had to be put down.

That much is still the case today. For a handgun, I'd forget the old Colt .45 thumb buster. The caliber's good, but the gun is limiting. Sure looks good, though. What I recommend is one of those revolvers or single shot handguns chambered for both the .410 bore shotgun and .45 Colt. The .410 may be the best snake getter ever designed, and the .45 is for everything else. The .410 can also be used for rabbits, squirrels and quail in a pinch. I'd get a gun that chambers the 3-inch .410 shell. Have a look at these: http://www.taurususa.com/gun-selector-results.cfm?series=41 .

One of the most fun things to do is to take a horse along on a deer hunt. It sure saves walking to camp and packing out meat on your back. So a cowboy who likes to hunt needs a rifle. The time-worn method is to take a Winchester, Savage or Marlin lever action along in a saddle scabbard. With the rifle butt toward the rear of the horse, of course.

But most deer hunters today prefer a longer rifle with a scope on it. There are scabbards made that will fit nearly every rifle these days. My own is a single-shot .45-70. My advice is to not buy a rifle specifically for horseback use, but one you're comfortable using on game. Then figure a way of carrying it on the horse.

One alternative is taking along a short shotgun that shoots slugs as well as buckshot and birdshot. One of the best is the UTS-15. Here's their address: www.utas-usa.com .

When you see a buck or bull elk you want to collect, dismount and tie your horse first, then take your shot.

Revolver. Courtesy of Creative Commons CC0.

11. Take a Shot at Mounted Archery

If you like horses and you like to fling sharp sticks, take a flyer in mounted archery. You can take lessons in Bend, Oregon, at the Cascade International Mounted Archery Center. First they teach you to shoot a bow from the ground, then from a horse being led.

When you're ready for world competition (oh yes … Hungary, Poland and Korea seem to be the hotbeds for this) you'll be able to put your horse into a run and shoot targets on either side of him. The beginner lessons are $74. All equipment is furnished. Lessons are in conjunction with the Bend Parks and Recreation folks. Call them at (541) 389-7275, or email for more information at info@cascademountedarchery.com. — www.cascademountedarchery.com

Arrows. Courtesy of Creative Commons CC0.

10. Attend Bob King's Cowboy School

Pay close attention at Bob King's Cowboy School. Well, what if riding broncs and driving cattle and riding across an Alp is a bit beyond your abilities? Hey, there's Bob King's Cowboy School in Cochise in southern Arizona. Bob can show you how it's done in a friendly manner, and he says you'll be able to go home and help local ranchers chouse the stock around and help out when you're done. Seriously, Bob makes it look like fun. Horse care, riding skills, roping, all the things a cowboy needs to know. There's never any substitute for experience, but this could be a fun way to get a start.

Reach Bob at (888) 596-3304 or email at cowboyschool@vtc.net. — www.cowboyschool.net

Wagon, San Antonio, TX. Courtesy of Barbe Awalt.

9. Wear a Wild Rag

Buy (and wear) a Wild Rag – and you will lose points if you mistakenly call it a bandana … which it ain't. And cowboy, if you ever refer to it as a scarf, may every nano-bit of testosterone you possess dry up and blow away forever in the next dust devil to come along.

Yes, it's silk. Yes, it feels good on the skin. Yes, it's for men. Get over it! (I'm partial to paisley myself). National Ropers Supply has a good selection. — http://nrsworld.com/

Wild rags. Courtesy of Creative Commons CC0.

8. Get Some Good Cowboy Boots

Price is sometimes a good indicator of a good pair of cowboy boots and sometimes it isn't. It *is* … when you've been properly fitted *before* the boots are made. It *isn't* … when you're buying boots off the rack but they're made of expensive stuff like defunct, endangered lizards or have jewels embedded in the toe.

The finest boots are made for *you*. Period. Years back I interviewed a famous bootmaker who had returned to his home at Jemez Pueblo after a full career in Chicago. He opened a drawer and pulled out bundles of cardboard cutouts in the shape of feet. He showed me some that belonged to movie stars and rock music legends. Each had drawn around each of their feet and sent it to him and the boots were made accordingly. Each of your feet, he told me, is slightly different from the other, so one size does *not* fit all.

But if you don't have enough money to pay off the national debt of a banana republic somewhere, here's a tip: buy a pair of boots "off the rack" at a good Western store, make sure they're comfortable *in the store*, and remember to get the best quality you can without any fancy foo-foos. Don't even consider a pair of boots that rub you wrong in the store. I don't care how good they look. You're going to be walking many more miles in them than you will be riding in them, no matter what you do for a living.

Now if you're an actual working cowboy (translation: poor to broke) here's a tip: go haunt some thrift stores and check out their boots. Sooner or later they'll have a pair in your size, that are affordable, and are ALREADY BROKEN IN! (Like mine…)

Expect to pay anywhere from $90 to $200 for readymade new boots from a good store. One of the good ones is Boot

Barn. Check them out at https://www.bootbarn.com/. But remember, just because you wear a size 10 and you're a "with it" modern cyber cowboy, do NOT order boots on the internet. Go in the store and try them on.

Fancy cowboy boots. Courtesy of Dreamstime.com ©julioaldana.

7. Join a Wagon Train

There are a handful of wagon trains you could join each summer, either as a driver (if you have your own wagon and team), a passenger (of course you have to agree to dress old timey) or an outrider (meaning you ride your own horse next to the wagons). These vary in length from four hours a day, ending up back where you started, to a monumental cross-country trek that will take three summers. That sounds like more fun, so get hold of wagonmaster Ben Kern and sign up.

You can ride ol' Snort from sea to shining sea, beginning in North Carolina and ending up in Oregon, or you can ride along with them just as they travel through your state, or just for one summer's worth, about 1,000 miles. If you go the whole 3,200 miles, you'll have gone twice as far as the Lewis and Clark Expedition did. But they couldn't stop at a drive-up window in Kentucky, of course.

For more information, call Ben Kern at (307) 234-9437 or email him at theaawt@hotmail.com. — http://allamericanwagontrain.com/index.php

On the Buckboard with Slim Randles and "Wild Horse Harry" Touloumis. Courtesy of the author.

6. Fix a Dutch Oven Dinner

The old cast-iron Dutch ovens were the range cook's best friends then, and they still are. They weigh a ton, it's really hard to ruin a meal in them, and they forgive all kinds of mistakes. Here's one meal I used to fix while guiding hunters in Alaska. In the morning, dig a hole about two feet deep. Dump in some coals from the wood-burning stove. Put a roast in the oven, along with potatoes, carrots, garlic (I don't like onions, but if you do ....) and a can of beer. (Pour it into the Dutch oven, don't set the can itself ... aw, you know). Put the lid on the oven and set it in the hole on top of the coals. Then dump more coals on top of the oven. Cover those coals with a piece of metal (I liked using the lid off a five-gallon paint can) and cover with dirt.

Come back in six hours, ten hours, twelve hours or tomorrow morning. Pop the lid on that thing and you're in business.

For more Dutch oven recipes: http://www.dutchovendude.com/dutch-oven-recipes.asp.

CHUCK WAGON GATHERING. *Photo by Joe Ownbey (www.ownbeyphotography.com). Courtesy of National Cowboy & Western Heritage Museum.*

5. Visit Parker Ranch

Put away the surfboard, rent a car and drive to the Parker Ranch. On the big island of Hawaii rests one of America's oldest and largest cattle ranches: the Parker Ranch. Go visit this 150,000-acre piece of paradise, full of 30,000 head of cattle, all pushed around correctly by *paniolos*, Hawaiian cowboys. The ranch had humble beginnings, when John Palmer Parker bought 10 acres of land on Hawaii from King Kamehameha in 1816. Then he married the king's daughter and his prospects started looking up. Cattle had run wild all over the island ever since Georges Vancouver gave some seasick longhorns to the king. Parker got permission from his in-laws to go catch some, and this began a thriving cattle business. Parker imported Mexican cowboys to work the cattle and they taught the locals how to rope and ride. They also introduced the guitar and ukulele to Hawaiian culture. This was in 1832, decades before cattle ranching got much of a foothold in the American West. — http://www.gohawaii.com/en/big-island/guidebook/topics/paniolo/

RANCH HAND. Courtesy of Creative Commons CC0.

4. Ride Around Iceland

Go visit the land of active volcanoes, short and shaggy horses and very tall blond people. There are several outfits that can fix you up and do this regularly. The people as well as the horses have been there since "settlement," which was about 1200 years ago. In fact, they take such pride in the purity of their horses' bloodlines that once an Icelandic horse leaves the country, he can never return, and no outside horses are allowed to visit there. These little horses are so short ... (How short are they, Slim?) ... if you wore spurs, you'd have training wheels. I've spent a few days in Iceland and can tell you these people are friendly, fluent in English, and the country is magnificent. I dare you to learn how to pronounce the names of the places you'll see.

Try these folks: Íshestar. Telephone (354) 555-7000 or email info@ishestar.is. They're based in Hafnarfjörður on Sörlaskeið Street. Let's see you pronounce that one. — http://www.ishestar.is/

Icelandic Horses. Courtesy of Creative Commons CC0.

3. Take a Rest at Little Lake, California

Located on U.S. 395 south of Olancha, the old rock-faced hotel burned down a few years back, and you can't even get a cup of coffee in this deserted place anymore, but it's worth a stop just to look at the little lake itself and beyond at the Coso Mountain Range. Closed to the public for years now as a Navy bombing range, the mountains hold some of the best-bred herds of wild horses in the world because an Olancha rancher, Mark Lacey, turned a retired racehorse stallion loose in there about 60 years ago.

For more information, and if you like wild horses, may I suggest reading *Sun Dog Days* by Slim Randles (that's me) a novel of mustanging that's about 90% true. I'll let you figure out which 10% I made up. — http://en.wikipedia.org/wiki/Little_Lake,_Inyo_County,_California; http://www.unmpress.com

Roping a Bronc. Courtesy of Jackie Cercek.

2. Sign Up for Bull Riding School

We saved this little goody for number two on the bucket list for obvious reasons. So what do you do the next time you're in North Canaan, Connecticut, that hotbed of rodeo action? Just saunter on over to the Let 'R Buck Bull Riding School and tell J.W. you'd like to throw your bull rope on one of his rankest. Don't forget to wear your helmet and flak vest. Cost? About $300, depending on a lot of stuff. — http://cnobull2tuff.com/

Bull riding. Courtesy of Bree Anderson-Burtis, Cheyenne Frontier Days.

1. And Finally, There's Bullfighting School

If you should happen to survive bull riding school in the wilds of Connecticut and your terror tank still isn't topped off, go on down to Branson, Missouri, and tell rodeo champ Lyle Sankey you'd like very much to dress up goofy, walk into a rodeo arena, and play slap and tickle with 2,000 pounds of mean. That's right, it's rodeo bullfighting school. They may look humorous (hey, we used to call them rodeo clowns, you know) but their work is deadly serious. They save lives, often by putting their own on the line.

What's it like? Okay, you're unarmed, standing in the arena, and there are two guys swinging baseball bats at you while the third waits to drive a car over you when they knock you down. There are good reasons why bullfighters wear track shoes.

If this sounds like fun, call Lyle at (417) 263-7777.

There's also a good reason why this is the last one on the bucket list. If you're anxious for more than these, you're one tough cowboy or cowgirl! — http://www.shop.sankeyrodeo.com/Rodeo-schools_c4.htm

BULLDOGGING AT 16 YRS. OLD, MONTEBELLO, CA. *Courtesy of the author.*

Some Last Words...

So there was this cowboy .... standing on the corner when he was approached by a tourist who just got off the bus.

"Excuse me, sir," said the tourist, "but are you a cowboy ... a real cowboy?"

"Well, I guess I am," the cowboy said, with a smile. "I've worked on ranches all my life, actually."

"There's some things I always wondered about," the tourist said, "and would you mind if I asked you about them?"

"No, I guess not..."

"Well, why do you fellas wear those big hats like you do?"

"Oh ... well, it keeps the sun off our faces in summer and keeps the rain and snow off in winter. Also, we can fill them with water and give the horse a drink."

"Whattya know about that," the tourist said. "And those leather things you wear on your legs?"

"Oh, those are chaps, and they protect our legs from thorns and brush when we're riding."

"I see," he said. "And why are you wearing sneakers instead of cowboy boots?"

And the cowboy looked at him and said softly, "Well, you wouldn't want people to think I was a truck driver, would ya?"

Route 66 mural. Courtesy of New Mexico True.

Near Misses . . .

Attend the WNFR (Wrangler National Finals Rodeo) in Las Vegas —*Melody Groves*

Be in or attend a Ranch Rodeo (different from a regular rodeo) —*Melody Groves*

Check out the following Kansas cowtowns: Abilene, Ellsworth, Caldwell, Wichita and Dodge City — *Johnny Boggs*

Do the Cotton-Eyed Joe or Dance a two-step —*Melody Groves*

Drive or own a pickup (should be white) with a bale of hay in the back —*Melody Groves*

Find a guest ranch that puts on cattle drives (real drives; that's right, you pay them to do their work) and see what it's really like pushin' little dogies — *Johnny Boggs*

Get a pair of Paul Bond boots. Bond started out breaking broncs for the cavalry at Carlsbad, New Mexico, and made a name for himself as a custom bookmaker in Nogales, Arizona. He made boots for working cowboys, movie cowboys and many others for almost 70 years, and though he died in 2012, his legacy lives on — *Johnny Boggs*

Know how to shoot a single action six revolver (mine is a Ruger, but a Colt Walker will do, too) —*Melody Groves*

Listen to Bob Wills and the Playboys play Western Swing —*Melody Groves*

Pony up for a unique week-long trail ride with Great American Adventures (http://great-american-adventures.com) in Santa Fe, Durango, Las Vegas, Palo Duro Canyon, Tombstone, or Monument Valley — *Paul Rhetts*

Listen to the music of Steve Cormier — *Slim Randles*

Spend a weekend at Texas' Cowboy Capital, Bandera, for bootscootin', beer-drinkin', cowboy-watchin' fun — *Johnny Boggs*

Spend the night at The Virginian Hotel — yes, it's named after Owen Wister's classic cowboy novel and opened in 1911, less than a decade after the book was first published — in Medicine Bow, Wyoming, the Virginian's old stamping grounds — *Johnny Boggs*

Take in the sights in Tombstone, Arizona—be sure to visit the O.K. Corral —*Melody Groves*

Tour the mansion of the original Hollywood cowboy, William S. Hart, in Newhall, California. Then watch *Hell's Hinges* and *Tumbleweeds* on your DVD player — *Johnny Boggs*

Treat yourself to custom-made cowboy hats from Rand's Custom Hats in Billings, Montana, and Greeley Hat Works in Greeley, Colorado — *Johnny Boggs*

INDIAN DANCES. *Courtesy of Bree Anderson-Burtis, Cheyenne Frontier Days.*

Cowboy Music

Top Western Songs list (in no particular order):

Home On The Range (Dr. Brewster Higley & Dan Kelly)
Whoopie Ti Yi Yo (*Git Aong Little Dogies*) (anonymous)
Little Joe The Wrangler (Jack Thorp)
Cool Water (Bob Nolan)
Tumbling Tumbleweeds (Bob Nolan)
Happy Trails (Dale Evans)
Doggone Cowboy (Joe Babcock)
Night Rider's Lament (Michael Burton)
The Cowboy Song (Roy Robinson)
Strawberry Roan (Curly Fletcher)
Old Chisholm Trail (anonymous)
Hell In Texas (anonymous)
El Paso (Marty Robbins)
My Heroes Have Always Been Cowboys (Sharon Vaughn)
The Last Roundup (Billy Hill)
This Ain't The Same Old Range (Bob Nolan)
Ragtime Cowboy Joe (Grant Clarke, Lewis F. Muir & Maurice Abrahams)
Navajo Rug (Ian Tyson & Tom Russell)
Cattle Call (Tex Owens)
Goodbye Old Paint (anonymous)
I Ride An Old Paint (anonymous)
(Ghost) Riders In The Sky (Stan Jones)
It's The West (Dave Stamey)
The Vaquero Song (Dave Stamey)
Red River Valley (anonymous)
Streets of Laredo (lyrics by Francis Henry Maynard)
Below The Kinney Rim (Michael Fleming & Les Buffham)
Tyin' Knots In The Devil's Tail (a.k.a. *The Sierry Petes*) (Gail Gardiner)
Wagon Wheels (Billy Hill)
Riding' Down The Canyon (Smiley Burnett & Gene Autry)
Back In The Saddle Again (Ray Whitley & Gene Autry)
I'm An Old Cowhand (Johnny Mercer)
Desperado (Glen Fry & Don Henley)
Can You Hear Those Pioneers (Rex Allen, Jr. & Judy Maude)
Colorado Trail (James A. Bliss)
Along The Navajo Trail (Larry Markes, Dick Charles & Eddie deLange)

Texas Plains (Stuart Hamblin)
I Wanta Be A Cowboy's Sweetheart (Patsy Montana)
Timber Trail (Tim Spencer)
Bury Me Not On The Lone Prairie (anonymous)
Carry Me Back To The Lone Prairie (Carson Robison)
The Goodnight Loving Trail (Utah Phillips)
When It's Springtime In The Rockies (Mary Hale Woolsey, Robert Sauer & Milt Taggart)
I'd Like To Be In Texas When They Round Up In The Spring (Carl Copeland & Jack Williams)
South Of The Border (Jimmy Kennedy & Michael Carr)
Don't Fence Me In (Cole Porter from a poem by Robert H. Fletcher)
Sweet Betsy From Pike (John A. Stone from "Villikens & His Dinah")
Amarillo By Morning (Terry Stafford & Paul Fraser)
Rhinestone Cowboy (Larry Weiss)
Along The Santa Fe Trail (Al Dubin, Edwina Coolidge & Will Grosz)
Cimarron (Johnny Bond)
Oklahoma Hills (Woody Guthrie & Jack Guthrie)
Empty Saddles (Billy Hill from a poem by J. Keirn Brennan)
The Hills Of Old Wyoming (Leo Robin & Ralph Rainger)
Banks Of The Sunny San Juan (Eddie Dean)
From Whence Came The Cowboy (Jack Hannah)
Great American Cowboy (Jack Hannah)
My Adobe Hacienda (Louise Massey & Lee Penny)
Arizona Waltz (Rex Allen, Sr.)
Ride, Cowboy, Ride (Denny deMarco, Rex Allen, Jr. & Curtis Allen)
When The Bloom Is On The Sage (Nat Vincent & Fred Howard)
Call Of The Wild (Rusty Richards)
Fence Rider (Rusty Richards)
The Gift (Ian Tyson)
The Same River (Juni Fisher)
Long May You Ride (Jim Jones)
You Just Can't See Him From The Road (Donnie Blanz)
Donny Catch A Horse For Me (R.W. Hampton)
Cross The Brazos At Waco (Kay Arnold)
Big Iron (Marty Robbins)
Mamas Don't Let Your Babies Grow Up To Be Cowboys (Ed Bruce & Patsy Bruce

—Rick Huff, Executive Vice President, Western Music Association

Cowboy Movies

Stage Coach (1939), directed by John Ford and starred John Wayne, John Carradine, Claire Trevor and Andy Devine. This film established Wayne as a major actor although he had previously appeared in several low-budget movies. The remakes of *Stage Coach* didn't measure up to the original.

The Westerner (1940), directed by William Wyler and starred Gary Cooper and Walter Brennan. A fine movie because of the quality of the stars. It is based on a story written by Stuart Lake, who also wrote Wyatt Earp's biography (such as it is).

The Gunfighter (1950), directed by Henry King and starred Gregory Peck. Many consider this the first "adult" Western.

High Noon (1952), directed by Fred Zinnemann and starred Gary Cooper, Grace Kelly and Katy Jurado. A fine movie. John Wayne didn't like it, but the film won four Academy Awards including a best actor nod for Cooper. Katy Jurado is excellent as Cooper's former love interest.

Magnificent Seven (1960), directed by John Sturges and starred Yul Brenner, Steve McQueen, Charles Bronson, Robert Vaughn, James Coburn, Horst Buchholz and Brad Dexter as the title seven. It also starred Eli Wallach. Based on the Japanese drama, *The Seven Samurai*, it is among the best American Westerns ever made. (None of the several sequels measure up to the original.)

The Man Who Shot Liberty Valance (1962) directed by John Ford and starred John Wayne, Lee Marvin and James Stewart. This is a great film based largely on the quality of the cast.

Cat Ballou (1965), directed by Elliot Silverstein and starred Jane Fonda and Lee Marvin. Marvin won an Academy Award for best actor.

The Good, the Bad and the Ugly (1966), directed by Sergio

Leone and starred Clint Eastwood, Eli Wallach and Lee Van Cleef. The last of Leone's westerns, it was a significant commercial success in that it cost just over $1 million to make and enjoyed a box office return of more than $25 million.

THE WILD BUNCH (1969), directed by Sam Peckinpah and starred William Holden, Ernest Borgnine, Edmond O'Brien, Robert Ryan, Warren Oates, Ben Johnson, Jaime Sánchez, L. Q. Jones and Emilio Fernández. While this film has been condemned by some for its extreme violence, others consider it the first Western to introduce realism into the Western film genre. It is historian Don Bullis' favorite western.

PAT GARRETT AND BILLY THE KID (1973), directed by Sam Peckinpah and starred James Coburn, Kris Kristofferson, Bob Dylan and Katy Jurado. The movie is historically incorrect on many points, but it includes one of the most touching scenes in all Westerns: it features Katy Jurado mourning the death of her husband, who had been shot down by outlaws (background music by Bob Dylan singing *Knockin' on Heaven's Door*). The cast makes the film otherwise worthwhile.

LITTLE BIG MAN (1970) directed by Arthur Penn and starred Dustin Hoffman, Faye Dunaway, Chief Dan George and Richard Milligan. The film is a satire which pokes fun at many of the legends of the Old West which are so dearly, and ardently, believed. It is based on a novel by Thomas Berger.

LONELY ARE THE BRAVE (1962) directed by David Miller and starred Kirk Douglas, Gena Rowlands and Walter Matthau. This movie is set in and around "Duke City", New Mexico. It involves a middle-aged cowboy who has outlived his time, and in some ways his usefulness, as he attempts to do one last good thing by breaking his friend out of jail. Douglas considered this one of his favorite films.

—Don Bullis, Official New Mexico Centennial Author

Build Your Own Bucket List

1.
2.
3.
4.
5.
6.
7.
8.
9.
10.
11.
12.
13.
14.
15.
16.
17.
18.
19.
20.
21.
22.
23.
24.
25.
26.
27.
28.
29.
30.
31.
32.

33.
34.
35.
36.
37.
38.
39.
40.
41.
42.
43.
44.
45.
46.
47.
48.
49.
50.
51.
52.
53.
54.
55.
56.
57.
58.
59.
60.
61.
62.
63.
64.
65.
66.

67.
68.
69.
70.
71.
72.
73.
74.
75.
76.
77.
78.
79.
80.
81.
82.
83.
84.
85.
86.
87.
88.
89.
90.
91.
92.
93.
94.
95.
96.
97.
98.
99.
100.

Cowboy Up! Horses for Heroes

Cowboy Up! is a unique horsemanship, wellness and skill-set restructuring program based in Santa Fe, New Mexico, free to ALL Operation Iraqi Freedom & Operation Enduring Freedom-Afghanistan, Operation New Dawn veterans and active military (both men and women), especially those who have sustained PTSD, combat trauma, or physical injuries during their time serving our country.

From day one, veterans are hands on with our horses beginning with groundwork and progressing to riding, as well as participating in other aspects of ranch life, including working cattle and more importantly experiencing the camaraderie with cowboys who are veterans themselves.

Sharing our experience, our strengths, and hopes, we give veterans a new and vital mission where they can recuperate, recreate, and reintegrate into the community. We believe that Horsemanship is Leadership and by assisting veterans through the way of the horse and cowboy culture, they are able to support their journey, integrating mind, body and spirit.

We are honored to be endorsed by the New Mexico Cattle Growers Association and their member ranches, Working Ranch Cowboys Association, (WRCA) and NM Department of Veterans' Services.

ABOUT THE AUTHOR

Slim Randles learned mule packing from Gene Burkhart and Slim Nivens. He learned mustanging and wild burro catching from Hap Pierce and horse shoeing from Rocky Earick. He learned horse training from Dick Johnson and Joe Cabral. He learned humility from the mules of the eastern High Sierra. For the last 40 years or so, he's written a lot of stuff, too, especially in his *Home Country* column, which is syndicated all across the world to over 4 million readers. He lives in Albuquerque, New Mexico, and in a small cabin in the middle of nowhere at the foot of the Manzano Mountains. Slim received the Rounders Award in 2012.

Other books by Slim Randles:

Ol' Jimmy Dollar, Rio Grande Books, 2015
Max Evans and a Few Friends, Rio Grande Books, 2014
Saddle Up! A Cowboy Guide to Writing, Rio Grande Books, 2014
The Backpocket Guide to Hunting Elk, Practical Advice from a Guide and Outfitter, Kindle e-book, 2014
Strange Tales of Alaska, Kindle e-book, 2014
Home Country, Rio Grande Books, 2012
A Cowboy's Guide to Growing Up Right, Rio Grande Books, 2011
Sweetgrass Mornings, University of New Mexico Press, 2011
Ol' Slim's Views from the Porch, New Mexico Magazine, 2007
Sun Dog Days, University of New Mexico Press, 2006
Ol' Max Evans, the First Thousand Years, University of New Mexico Press, 2004
Hot Biscuits, University of New Mexico Press, 2002
Raven's Prey, McRoy and Blackburn, 1998
The Long Dark, An Alaska Winter's Tale, Alaska Northwest Publishing, 1984 and 2003
Hell, I Was There! The life story of Elmer Keith, Petersen Publishing, 1979
Dogsled, A True Tale of the North, Winchester Press, 1977.

CPSIA information can be obtained at www.ICGtesting.com
Printed in the USA
LVIW01n0458110915
453560LV00001B/1